PYTHON FOR
DATA SCIENCE

Guide to computer programming and web
coding. Learn machine learning, artificial
intelligence, NumPy and Pandas packages for
data analysis. Step-by-step exercises included.

JASON TEST

TABLE OF CONTENT

INTRODUCTION

D ata Science has been very popular over the last couple of years. The main focus of this sector is to incorporate significant data into business and marketing strategies that will help a business expand. And get to a logical solution, the data can be stored and explored. Originally only the leading IT corporations were engaged throughout this field, but today information technology is being used by companies operating in different sectors and fields such as e-commerce, medical care, financial services, and others. Software processing programs such as Hadoop, R code, SAS, SQL, and plenty more are available. Python is, however, the most famous and easiest to use data and analytics tools. It is recognized as the coding world's Swiss Army Knife since it promotes structured coding, object-oriented programming, the operational programming language, and many others. Python is the most widely used programming language in the world and is also recognized as the most high - level language for data science tools and techniques, according to the 2018 Stack Overflow study.

In the Hacker rank 2018 developer poll, which is seen in their love-hate ranking, Python has won the developer's hearts. Experts in data science expect to see an increase in the Python ecosystem, with growing popularity. And although your journey to study Python programming may just start, it's nice to know that there are also plentiful (and increasing) career options.

Data analytics Python programming is extensively used and, along with being a flexible and open-source language, becomes one of the favorite programming languages. Its large libraries are used for data processing, and even for a beginner data analyst, they are very easy to understand. Besides being open-source, it also integrates easily with any infrastructure that can be used to fix the most complicated problems. It is used by most banks for data crunching, organizations for analysis and processing, and weather prediction firms such as Climate monitor analytics often use it. The annual wage for a Computer Scientist is $127,918, according to Indeed. So here's the good news, the figure is likely to increase. IBM's experts forecast a 28 percent increase in data scientists' demands by 2020. For data science, however, the future is bright, and Python is just one slice of the golden pie. Luckily mastering Python and other principles of programming are as practical as ever.

DATA SCIENCE AND ITS SIGNIFICANCE

Data Science has come a long way from the past few years, and thus, it becomes an important factor in understanding the workings of multiple companies. Below are several explanations that prove data science will still be an integral part of the global market.

1. The companies would be able to understand their client in a more efficient and high manner with the help of Data Science. Satisfied customers form the foundation of every company, and they play an important role in their successes or failures. Data Science allows companies to engage with customers in the advance way and thus proves the product's improved performance and strength.

2. Data Science enables brands to deliver powerful and engaging visuals. That's one of the reasons it's famous. When products and companies make inclusive use of this data, they can share their experiences with their audiences and thus create better relations with the item.

3. Perhaps one Data Science's significant characteristics are that its results can be generalized to almost all kinds of industries, such as travel, health care, and education. The companies can quickly determine their problems with the help of Data Science, and can also adequately address them

4. Currently, data science is accessible in almost all industries, and nowadays, there is a huge amount of data existing in the world, and if used adequately, it can lead to victory or failure of any project. If data is used properly, it will be important in the future to achieve the product 's goals.

5. Big data is always on the rise and growing. Big data allows the enterprise to address complicated Business, human capital, and capital management problems effectively and quickly using different resources that are built routinely.

6. Data science is gaining rapid popularity in every other sector and therefore plays an important role in every product's functioning and performance. Thus, the data scientist's role is also enhanced as they will conduct an essential function of managing data and providing solutions to particular issues.

7. Computer technology has also affected the supermarket sectors. To understand this, let's take an example the older people had a fantastic interaction with the local seller. Also, the seller was able to meet the customers' requirements in a personalized way. But now this attention was lost due to the emergence and increase of supermarket chains. But the sellers are able to communicate with their customers with the help of data analytics.

8. Data Science helps companies build that customer connection. Companies and their goods will be able to have a better and deeper understanding of how clients can utilize their services with the help of data science.

Data Technology Future: Like other areas are continually evolving, the importance of data technology is increasingly growing as well. Data science impacted different fields. Its influence can be seen in many industries, such as retail, healthcare, and education. New treatments and technologies are being continually identified in the healthcare sector, and there is a need for quality patient care. The healthcare industry can find a solution with the help of data science techniques that helps the patients to take care with. Education is another field where one can clearly see the advantage of data science. Now the new innovations like phones and tablets have become an essential characteristic of the educational system. Also, with the help of data science, the students are creating greater chances, which leads to improving their knowledge.

Data Science Life Cycle:

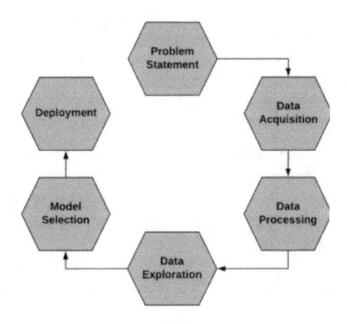

Data Structures

A data structure may be selected in computer programming or designed to store data for the purpose of working with different algorithms on it. Every other data structure includes the data values, data relationships, and functions between the data that can be applied to the data and information.

Features of data structures

Sometimes, data structures are categorized according to their characteristics. Possible functions are:

- Linear or non-linear: This feature defines how the data objects are organized in a sequential series, like a list or in an unordered sequence, like a table.
- Homogeneous or non-homogeneous: This function defines how all data objects in a collection are of the same type or of different kinds.
- Static or dynamic: This technique determines to show to assemble the data structures. Static data structures at compilation time have fixed sizes, structures, and destinations in the memory. Dynamic data types have dimensions, mechanisms, and destinations of memory that may shrink or expand depending on the application.

Data structure Types

Types of the data structure are determined by what sorts of operations will be needed or what kinds of algorithms will be implemented. This includes:

Arrays: An array stores a list of memory items at adjacent locations. Components of the same category are located together since each element's position can be easily calculated or accessed. Arrays can be fixed in size or flexible in length.

Stacks: A stack holds a set of objects in linear order added to operations. This order may be past due in first out (LIFO) or first-out (FIFO).

Queues: A queue stores a stack-like selection of elements; however, the sequence of activity can only be first in the first out. Linked lists: In a linear order, a linked list stores a selection of items. In a linked list, every unit or node includes a data item as well as a reference or relation to the next element in the list.

Trees: A tree stocks an abstract, hierarchical collection of items. Each node is connected to other nodes and can have several sub-values, also known as a child.

Graphs: A graph stores a non-linear design group of items. Graphs consist of a limited set of nodes, also called vertices, and lines connecting them, also known as edges. They are useful for describing processes in real life, such as networked computers.

Tries: A tria or query tree is often a data structure that stores strings as data files, which can be arranged in a visual graph.

Hash tables: A hash table or hash chart is contained in a relational list that labels the keys to variables. A hash table uses a hashing algorithm to transform an index into an array of containers containing the desired item of data. These data systems are called complex because they can contain vast quantities of interconnected data. Examples of primal, or fundamental, data structures are integer, float, boolean, and character.

Utilization of data structures

Data structures are generally used to incorporate the data types in physical forms. This can be interpreted into a wide range of applications, including a binary tree showing a database table. Data structures are used in the programming languages to organize code and information in digital storage. Python databases and dictionaries, or

JavaScript array and objects, are popular coding systems used to gather and analyze data. Also, data structures are a vital part of effective software design. Significance of Databases Data systems is necessary to effectively handle vast volumes of data, such as data stored in libraries, or indexing services.

Accurate data configuration management requires memory allocation identifier, data interconnections, and data processes, all of which support the data structures. In addition, it is important to not only use data structures but also to select the correct data structure for each assignment.

Choosing an unsatisfactory data structure could lead to slow running times or disoriented code. Any considerations that need to be noticed when choosing a data system include what type of information should be processed, where new data will be put, how data will be organized, and how much space will be allocated for the data.

PYTHON BASICS

You can get all the knowledge about the Python programming language in 5 simple steps.

Step 1: Practice Basics in Python

It all starts somewhere. This first step is where the basics of programming Python will be learned. You are always going to want an introduction to data science. Jupyter Notebook, which comes pre-portioned with Python libraries to help you understand these two factors, which make it one of the essential resources which you can start using early on your journey.

Step 2: Try practicing Mini-Python Projects

We strongly believe in learning through shoulders-on. Try programming stuff like internet games, calculators, or software that gets Google weather in your area. Creating these mini-projects can help you understand Python. Projects like these are standard for any coding languages, and a fantastic way to strengthen your working knowledge. You will come up with better and advance API knowledge, and you will continue site scraping with advanced techniques. This will enable you to learn Python programming more effectively, and the web scraping method will be useful to you later when collecting data.

Stage 3: Learn Scientific Libraries on Python

Python can do anything with data. Pandas, Matplotliband, and NumPyare are known to be the three best used and most important Python Libraries for data science. NumPy and Pandas are useful for data creation and development. Matplotlib is a library for analyzing the data, creating flow charts and diagrams as you would like to see in Excel or Google Sheets.

Stage 4: Create a portfolio

A portfolio is an absolute need for professional data scientists. These projects must include numerous data sets and leave important perspectives to readers that you have gleaned. Your portfolio does not have a specific theme; finding datasets that inspire you, and then finding a way to place them together. Showing projects like these provide some collaboration to fellow data scientists, and demonstrates future employers that you have really taken the chance to understand Python and other essential coding skills. Some of the good things about data science are that, while showcasing the skills you've learned, your portfolio serves as a resume, such as Python programming.

Step 5: Apply Advanced Data Science Techniques

Eventually, the target is to strengthen your programming skills. Your data science path will be full of continuous learning, but you can accomplish specialized tutorials to make sure you have specialized in the basic programming of Python. You need to get confident with clustering models of regression, grouping, and k-means. You can also leap into machine learning-using sci-kit lessons to bootstrap models and create neural network models. At this point, developer programming could include creating models using live data sources.

10

This type of machine learning technique adjusts s its assumptions over time.

How significant is Python for Data Science?

Efficient and simple to use – Python is considered a tool for beginners, and any student or researcher with only basic understanding could start working on it. Time and money spent debugging codes and constraints on different project management are also minimized. The time for code implementation is less compared to other programming languages such as C, Java, and C #, which makes developers and software engineers spend far more time working on their algorithms.

Library Choice-Python offers a vast library and machine learning and artificial intelligence database. Scikit Learn, TensorFlow, Seaborn, Pytorch, Matplotlib, and many more are among the most popular libraries. There are many online tutorial videos and resources on machine learning and data science, which can be easily obtained.

Scalability – Python has proven itself to be a highly scalable and faster language compared to other programming languages such as c++, Java, and R. It gives flexibility in solving problems that can't be solved with other computer languages. Many companies use it to develop all sorts of rapid techniques and systems.

#Visual Statistics and Graphics-Python provides a number of visualization tools. The Matplotlib library provides a reliable framework on which those libraries such as gg plot, pandas plotting, PyTorch, and others are developed. These services help create graphs, plot lines ready for the Web, visual layouts, etc.

How Python is used for Data Science

#First phase – First of all, we need to learn and understand what form a data takes. If we perceive data to be a huge Excel sheet with columns and crows lakhs, then perhaps you should know what to do about that? You need to gather information into each row as well as column by executing some operations and searching for a specific type of data. Completing this type of computational task can consume a lot of time and hard work. Thus, you can use Python's libraries, such as Pandas and Numpy, that can complete the tasks quickly by using parallel computation.

#Second phase – The next hurdle is to get the data needed. Since data is not always readily accessible to us, we need to dump data from the network as needed. Here the Python Scrap and brilliant Soup libraries can enable us to retrieve data from the internet.

#Third phase – We must get the simulation or visual presentation of the data at this step. Driving perspectives gets difficult when you have too many figures on the board. The correct way to do that is to represent the data in graph form, graphs, and other layouts. The Python Seaborn and Matplotlib libraries are used to execute this operation.

#Fourth phase – The next stage is machine-learning, which is massively complicated computing. It includes mathematical tools such as the probability, calculus, and matrix operations of columns and rows over lakhs. With Python's machine learning library Scikit-Learn, all of this will become very simple and effective.

Standard Library

The Python Standard library consists of Python's precise syntax, token, and semantic. It comes packaged with deployment core Python.

When we started with an introduction, we referenced this. It is written in C and covers features such as I / O and other core components. Together all of the versatility renders makes Python the language it is. At the root of the basic library, there are more than 200 key modules. Python ships that library. But aside from this library, you can also obtain a massive collection of several thousand Python Package Index (PyPI) components.

1. Matplotlib

'Matplotlib' helps to analyze data, and is a library of numerical plots. For Data Science, we discussed in Python.

2. Pandas

'Pandas' is a must for data-science as we have said before. It provides easy, descriptive, and versatile data structures to deal with organized (tabulated, multilayered, presumably heterogeneous) and series data with ease (and fluidly).

3. Requests

'Requests' is a Python library that allows users to upload HTTP/1.1 requests, add headers, form data, multipart files, and simple Python dictionary parameters. In the same way, it also helps you to access the response data.

4. NumPy

It has basic arithmetic features and a rudimentary collection of scientific computing.

5. SQLAlchemy

It has sophisticated mathematical features, and SQLAlchemy is a basic mathematical programming library with well-known trends at a corporate level. It was created to make database availability efficient and high-performance.

6. BeautifulSoup

This may be a bit on the slow side. BeautifulSoup seems to have a superb library for beginner XML- and HTML- parsing.

7. Pyglet

Pyglet is an outstanding choice when designing games with an object-oriented programming language interface. It also sees use in the development of other visually rich programs for Mac OS X, Windows, and Linux in particular. In the 90s, they turned to play Minecraft on their PCs whenever people were bored. Pyglet is the mechanism powering Minecraft.

8. SciPy

Next available is SciPy, one of the libraries we spoke about so often. It does have a range of numerical routines that are user-friendly and effective. Those provide optimization routines and numerical integration procedures.

9. Scrapy

If your objective is quick, scraping at the high-level monitor and crawling the network, go for Scrapy. It can be used for data gathering activities for monitoring and test automation.

10. PyGame

PyGame offers an incredibly basic interface to the system-independent graphics, audio, and input libraries of the Popular Direct Media Library (SDL).

11. Python Twisted

Twisted is an event-driven networking library used in Python and authorized under the MIT open-source license.

12. Pillow

Pillow is a PIL (Python Imaging Library) friendly fork but is more user efficient. Pillow is your best friend when you're working with pictures.

13. pywin32

As the name suggests, this gives useful methods and classes for interacting with Windows.

14. wxPython

For Python, it's a wrapper around wxWidgets.

15. iPython

iPython Python Library provides a parallel distributed computing architecture. You will use it to create, run, test, and track parallel and distributed programming.

16. Nose

The nose provides alternate test exploration and test automation running processes. This intends to mimic the behavior of the py.test as much as possible.

17. Flask

Flask is a web framework, with a small core and several extensions.

18. SymPy

It is a library of open-source symbolic mathematics. SymPy is a full-fledged Computer Algebra System (CAS) with a very simple and easily understood code that is highly expandable. It is implemented in python, and therefore, external libraries are not required.

19. Fabric

As well as being a library, Fabric is a command-line tool to simplify the use of SSH for installation programs or network management activities. You can run local or remote command line, upload/download files, and even request input user going, or abort activity with it.

20. PyGTK

PyGTK allows you to create programs easily using a Python GUI (Graphical User Interface).

Operators and Expressions

Operators

In Python, operators are special symbols that perform mathematical operation computation. The value in which the operator is running on is called the operand.

Arithmetic operators

It is used by arithmetic operators to perform mathematical operations such as addition, subtraction, multiplying, etc.

Comparison operators

Comparison operators can be used for value comparisons. Depending on the condition, it returns either True or False.

Logical operators

Logical operators are and, or, not.

Operator	Meaning	Example
And	True if both operands are true	x and y
Or	True if either of the operands is true	x or y
Not	True if the operand is false (complements the operand)	not x

Bitwise operators

Bitwise operators operate as if they became binary-digit strings on operands. Bit by bit they work, and therefore the name. For example, in binary two is10, and in binary seven is 111.

Assignment operators

Python language's assignment operators are used to assign values to the variables. a = 5 is a simple task operator assigning 'a' value of 5 to the right of the variable 'a' to the left. In Python, there are various compound operators such as a + = 5, which adds to the variable as well as assigns the same later. This equals a= a + 5.

Special operators

Python language gives other different types of operators, such as the operator of the identity or the operator of membership. Examples of these are mentioned below.

Identity operators

'Is' and 'is not' are Python Identity Operators. They are used to test if there are two values or variables in the same memory section. Two equal variables do not mean they are equivalent.

Membership operator

The operators that are used to check whether or not there exists a value/variable in the sequence such as string, list, tuples, sets, and dictionary. These operators return either True or False if a variable is found in the list, it returns True, or else it returns False

Expressions

An expression is a mix of values, variables, operators, and function calls. There must be an evaluation of the expressions. When you ask Python to print a phrase, the interpreter will evaluate the expression and show the output.

Arithmetic conversions

Whenever an arithmetic operator interpretation below uses the phrase "the numeric arguments are converted to a common type," this means the execution of the operator for the built-in modes operates as follows

If one argument is a complex quantity, then the other is converted to a complex number; If another argument is a floating-point number, the other argument is transformed to a floating-point; Or else both will be integers with no need for conversion.

Atoms

Atoms are the most important expressional components. The smallest atoms are literals or abstract identities. Forms contained in parentheses, brackets, or braces are also syntactically known as atoms. Atoms syntax is:

atom ::= identifier | enclosure| literal

enclosure ::= list_display| parenth_form| dict_display | set_display

Identifiers (Names)

A name is an identifier that occurs as an atom. See section Lexical Description Identifiers and Keywords and group Naming and binding for naming and binding documents. Whenever the name is connected to an entity, it yields the entity by evaluating the atom. When a name is not connected, an attempt to assess it elevates the exception for NameError.

Literals

Python provides logical string and bytes and numerical literals of different types:

literal::= string literal | bytes literal

| integer | float number | image number

Assessment of a literal yield with the predicted set an object of that type (bytes, integer, floating-point number, string, complex number). In the scenario of floating-point and imaginary (complex) literals, the value can be approximated.

Parenthesized forms

A parenthesized type is an available set of parentheses for the expression:

parenth_form ::= "(" [starred_expression] ")"

A list of parenthesized expressions yields whatever the list of expressions produces: if the list includes at least one comma, it produces a tuple. If not, it yields the sole expression that forms up the list of expressions. A null pair of parentheses generates an incomplete object of tuples. As all tuples are immutable, the same rules would apply as for literals (i.e., two empty tuple occurrences does or doesn't yield the same entity).

Displays for lists, sets, and dictionaries

For the construction of a list, Python uses a series or dictionary with a particular syntax called "displays," each in complementary strands: The contents of the container are listed explicitly, or They are calculated using a series of instructions for looping and filtering, named a 'comprehension.' Common features of syntax for comprehensions are:

comprehension ::= assignment_expressioncomp_for

comp_for   ::= ["async"] "for" target_list "in" or_test [comp_iter] comp_iter   ::= comp_for | comp_if

comp_if   ::= "if" expression_nocond [comp_iter]

A comprehension contains one single sentence ready for at least one expression for clause, and zero or more for or if clauses. Throughout this situation, the components of the container are those that will be generated by assuming each of the for or if clauses as a block, nesting from left to right, and determining the phase for creating an entity each time the inner core block is approached.

List displays

A list view is a probably empty sequence of square brackets including expressions:

list_display ::= "[" [starred_list | comprehension] "]"

A list display generates a new column object, with either a list of expressions or a comprehension specifying the items. When a comma-separated database of expressions is provided, its elements are assessed from left to right and positioned in that order in the category entity. When Comprehension is provided, the list shall be built from the comprehension components.

Set displays

Curly braces denote a set display and can be distinguished from dictionary displays by the lack of colons dividing data types:

set_display ::= "{" (starred_list | comprehension) "}"

A set show offers a new, mutable set entity, with either a series of expressions or a comprehension defining the contents. When supplied with a comma-separated list of expressions, its elements are evaluated from left to right and assigned to the set entity. Whenever a comprehension is provided, the set is formed from the comprehension-derived elements. Unable to build an empty set with this {}; literal forms a blank dictionary.

Dictionary displays

A dictionary view is a potentially empty sequence of key pairs limited to curly braces:

dict_display   ::= "{" [key_datum_list | dict_comprehension] "}"

key_datum_list   ::= key_datum ("," key_datum)* [","]

key_datum   ::= expression ":" expression | "**" or_expr

dict_comprehension ::= expression ":" expression comp_for

The dictionary view shows a new object in the dictionary. When a comma-separated series of key / datum pairs is provided, they are analyzed from left to right to identify dictionary entries: each key entity is often used as a key to hold the respective datum in the dictionary. This implies you can clearly state the very same key numerous times in the key /datum catalog, but the last one given will become the final dictionary's value for that key.

Generator expressions

A generator expression is the compressed syntax of a generator in the parenthesis :

generator_expression ::= "(" expression comp_for ")"

An expression generator produces an entity that is a new generator. Its syntax will be the same as for comprehensions, except for being enclosed in brackets or curly braces rather than parentheses. Variables being used generator expression are assessed sloppily when the generator object (in the same style as standard generators) is called by the __next__() method. Conversely, the iterate-able expression in the leftmost part of the clause is evaluated immediately, such that an error that it produces is transmitted at the level where the expression of the generator is characterized, rather than at the level where the first value is recovered.

For instance: (x*y for x in range(10) for y in range(x, x+10)).

Yield expressions

yield_atom   ::= "(" yield_expression ")"

yield_expression ::= "yield" [expression_list | "from" expression]

The produced expression is used to define a generator function or async generator function, and can therefore only be used in the function definition body. Using an expression of yield in the body of a function tends to cause that function to be a generator, and to use it in the body of an asynchronous def function induces that co-routine function to become an async generator. For example:

def gen(): # defines a generator function

yield 123

asyncdefagen(): # defines an asynchronous generator function

yield 123

Because of their adverse effects on the carrying scope, yield expressions are not allowed as part of the impliedly defined scopes used to enforce comprehensions and expressions of generators.

Input and Output of Data in Python

Python Output Using print() function

To display data into the standard display system (screen), we use the print() function. We may issue data to a server as well, but that will be addressed later. Below is an example of its use.

>>>>print('This sentence is output to the screen')

Output:

This sentence is output to the screen

Another example is given:

a = 5

print('The value of a is,' a)

Output:

The value of a is 5

Within the second declaration of print(), we will note that space has been inserted between the string and the variable value a. By default, it contains this syntax, but we can change it.

The actual syntax of the print() function will be:

print(*objects, sep=' ', end='\n', file=sys.stdout, flush=False)

Here, the object is the value(s) that will be printed. The sep separator between values is used. This switches into a character in space. Upon printing all the values, the finish is printed. It moves into a new section by design. The file is the object that prints the values, and its default value is sys.stdout (screen). Below is an example of this.

print(1, 2, 3, 4)

print(1, 2, 3, 4, sep='*')

print(1, 2, 3, 4, sep='#', end='&')

Run code

Output:

1 2 3 4

1*2*3*4

1#2#3#4&

Output formatting

Often we want to style our production, so it looks appealing. It can be done using the method str.format(). This technique is visible for any object with a string.

>>> x = 5; y = 10

>>>print('The value of x is {} and y is {}'.format(x,y))

Here the value of x is five and y is 10

Here, they use the curly braces{} as stand-ins. Using numbers (tuple index), we may specify the order in which they have been printed.

print('I love {0} and {1}'.format('bread','butter'))

print('I love {1} and {0}'.format('bread','butter'))

Run Code

Output:

I love bread and butter

I love butter and bread

People can also use arguments with keyword to format the string.

>>>print('Hello   {name},   {greeting}'.format(greeting   = 'Goodmorning', name = 'John'))

Hello John, Goodmorning

Unlike the old sprint() style used in the C programming language, we can also format strings. To accomplish this, we use the '%' operator.

>>> x = 12.3456789

>>>print('The value of x is %3.2f' %x)

The value of x is 12.35

>>>print('The value of x is %3.4f' %x)

The value of x is 12.3457

Python Indentation

Indentation applies to the spaces at the start of a line of the compiler. Whereas indentation in code is for readability only in other programming languages, but the indentation in Python is very important. Python supports the indent to denote a code block.

Example

if 5 > 2:

print("Five is greater than two!")

Python will generate an error message if you skip the indentation:

Example

Syntax Error:

if 5 > 2:

print("Five is greater than two!")

Python Input

Our programs have been static. Variables were described or hard-coded in the source code. We would want to take the feedback from the user to allow flexibility. We have the input() function in Python to enable this. input() is syntax as:

input([prompt])

While prompt is the string we want to show on the computer, this is optional.

>>>num = input('Enter a number: ')

Enter a number: 10

>>>num

'10'

Below, we can see how the value 10 entered is a string and not a number. To transform this to a number we may use the functions int() or float().

>>>int('10')

10

>>>float('10')

10.0

The same method can be done with the feature eval(). Although it takes eval much further. It can even quantify expressions, provided that the input is a string

>>>int('2+3')

Traceback (most recent call last):

  File "<string>", line 301, in runcode

  File "<interactive input>", line 1, in <module>

ValueError: int() base 10 invalid literal: '2+3'

>>>eval('2+3')

5

Python Import

As our software gets larger, splitting it up into separate modules is a smart idea. A module is a file that contains definitions and statements from Python. Python packages have a filename, and the .py extension begins with it. Definitions may be loaded into another module or to the integrated Python interpreter within a module. To do this, we use the keyword on import.

For instance, by writing the line below, we can import the math module:

import math

We will use the module as follows:

import math

print(math.pi)

Run Code

Output

3.141592653589793

So far, all concepts are included in our framework within the math module. Developers can also only import certain particular attributes and functions, using the keyword.

For instance:

>>>from math import pi

>>>pi

3.141592653589793

Python looks at multiple positions specified in sys.path during the import of a module. It is a list of positions in a directory.

>>> import sys

>>>sys.path

[",

'C:\\Python33\\Lib\\idlelib',

'C:\\Windows\\system32\\python33.zip',

'C:\\Python33\\DLLs',

'C:\\Python33\\lib',

'C:\\Python33',

'C:\\Python33\\lib\\site-packages']

We can insert our own destination to that list as well.

FUNCTIONS

You utilize programming functions to combine a list of instructions that you're constantly using or that are better self-contained in sub-program complexity and are called upon when required. Which means a function is a type of code written to accomplish a given purpose. The function may or may not need various inputs to accomplish that particular task. Whenever the task is executed, one or even more values can or could not be returned by the function. Basically there exist three types of functions in Python language:

1. Built-in functions, including help() to ask for help, min() to just get the minimum amount, print() to print an attribute to the terminal. More of these functions can be found here.
2. User-Defined Functions (UDFs) that are functions created by users to assist and support them out;
3. Anonymous functions, also labeled lambda functions since they are not defined with the default keyword.

Defining A Function: User Defined Functions (UDFs)

The following four steps are for defining a function in Python:

1. Keyword def can be used to declare the function and then use the function name to backtrack.
2. Add function parameters: They must be within the function parentheses. Finish off your line with a colon.
3. Add statements which should be implemented by the functions.

When the function should output something, end your function with a return statement. Your task must return an object None without return declaration. Example:

1. def hello():

2. print("Hello World")

3.return

It is obvious as you move forward, the functions will become more complex: you can include for loops, flow control, and more to make things more fine-grained:

def hello():

name = str(input("Enter your name: "))

if name:

print ("Hello " + str(name))

else:

print("Hello World")

return

hello()

In the feature above, you are asking the user to give a name. When no name is provided, the 'Hello World' function will be printed. Otherwise, the user will receive a custom "Hello" phrase. Also, consider you can specify one or more parameters for your UDFs function. When you discuss the segment Feature Statements, you will hear more about this. Consequently, as a result of your function, you may or may not return one or more values.

The return Statement

Note that since you're going to print something like that in your hello) (UDF, you don't really have to return it. There'll be no distinction between the above function and this one:

Example:

1. defhello_noreturn():

2. print("Hello World")

Even so, if you'd like to keep working with the result of your function and try a few other functions on it, you'll need to use the return statement to simply return a value, like a string, an integer. Check out the following scenario in which hello() returns a "hello" string while the hello_noreturn() function returns None:

1.   def hello():

2.   print("Hello World")

3.   return("hello")

4.   defhello_noreturn():

5.   print("Hello World")

6.   # Multiply the output of `hello()` with 2

7.   hello() * 2

8.   # (Try to) multiply the output of `hello_noreturn()` with 2

9.   hello_noreturn() * 2

The secondary part gives you an error because, with a None, you cannot perform any operations. You will get a TypeError that appears to say that NoneType (the None, which is the outcome of hello_noreturn()) and int (2) cannot do the multiplication operation. Tip functions leave instantly when a return statement is found, even though that means they will not return any result:

1. def run():

2. for x in range(10):

3. if x == 2:

4. return

5. print("Run!")

6.   run()

Another factor worth noting when dealing with the 'return expression' is many values can be returned using it. You consider making use of tuples for this. Recall that this data structure is very comparable to a list's: it can contain different values. Even so, tuples are immutable, meaning you can't alter any amounts stored in it! You build it with the aid of dual parentheses). With the assistance of the comma and the assignment operator, you can disassemble tuples into different variables.

Read the example below to understand how multiple values can be returned by your function:

1.   # Define `plus()`

2.   def plus(a,b):

3.sum = a + b

4.return (sum, a)

5.   # Call `plus()` and unpack variables

6.   sum, a = plus(3,4)

7.   # Print `sum()`

8.   print(sum)

Notice that the return statement sum, 'a' will result in just the same as the return (sum, a): the earlier simply packs total and an in a tuple it under hood!

How To Call A Function

You've already seen a lot of examples in previous sections of how one can call a function. Trying to call a function means executing the function you have described-either directly from the Python prompt, or by a different function (as you have seen in the "Nested Functions" portion). Call your new added hello() function essentially by implementing hello() as in the DataCamp Light chunk as follows:

1.   hello()

Adding Docstrings to Python Functions

Further valuable points of Python's writing functions: docstrings. Docstrings define what your function does, like the algorithms it conducts or the values it returns. These definitions act as metadata for your function such that anybody who reads the docstring of your feature can understand what your feature is doing, without having to follow all the code in the function specification. Task docstrings are placed right after the feature header in the subsequent line and are set in triple quote marks. For your hello() function, a suitable docstring is 'Hello World prints.'

```
def hello():

"""Prints "Hello World".

Returns:

    None

"""

print("Hello World")

return
```

Notice that you can extend docstrings more than the one provided here as an example. If you want to study docstrings in more depth information, you should try checking out some Python library Github repositories like scikit-learn or pandas, in which you'll find lots of good examples!

Function Arguments in Python

You probably learned the distinction between definitions and statements earlier. In simple terms, arguments are the aspects that are given to any function or method call, while their parameter identities respond to the arguments in the function or method code. Python UDFs can take up four types of arguments:

1. Default arguments
2. Required arguments
3. Keyword arguments
4. Variable number of arguments

Default Arguments

Default arguments would be those who take default data if no value of the argument is delivered during the call function. With the assignment operator =, as in the following case, you may assign this default value:

1. #Define `plus()` function

2. def plus(a,b = 2):

3.return a + b

4. # Call `plus()` with only `a` parameter

5. plus(a=1)

6. # Call `plus()` with `a` and `b` parameters

7. plus(a=1, b=3)

Required Arguments

Because the name sort of brings out, the claims a UDF needs are those that will be in there. Such statements must be transferred during the function call and are absolutely the right order, such as in the example below:

1. # Define `plus()` with required arguments

2. def plus(a,b):

3. return a + b

Calling the functions without getting any additional errors, you need arguments that map to 'a' as well as the 'b' parameters. The result will not be unique if you swap round the 'a' and 'b,' but it could be if you modify plus() to the following:

1. # Define `plus()` with required arguments

2. def plus(a,b):

3.return a/b

Keyword Arguments

You will use keyword arguments in your function call if you'd like to make sure you list all the parameters in the correct order. You use this to define the statements by the name of the function. Let's take an example above to make it a little simpler:

1. # Define `plus()` function

2. def plus(a,b):

3.return a + b

4. # Call `plus()` function with parameters

5. plus(2,3)

6. # Call `plus()` function with keyword arguments

7. plus(a=1, b=2)

Notice that you can also alter the sequence of the parameters utilizing keywords arguments and still get the same outcome when executing the function:

1. # Define `plus()` function

2. def plus(a,b):

3.return a + b

4. # Call `plus()` function with keyword arguments

5. plus(b=2, a=1)

Global vs. Local Variables

Variables identified within a function structure usually have a local scope, and those specified outside have a global scope. This shows that the local variables are specified within a function block and can only be retrieved through that function, while global variables can be retrieved from all the functions in the coding:

1. # Global variable `init`

2. init = 1

3. # Define `plus()` function to accept a variable number of arguments

4. def plus(*args):

5. # Local variable `sum()`

6.total = 0

7.fori in args:

8.total += i

9.return total

10.# Access the global variable

11.print("this is the initialized value " + str(init))

12.# (Try to) access the local variable

13.print("this is the sum " + str(total))

You will find that you can get a NameError that means the name 'total' is not specified as you attempt to print out the total local variable that was specified within the body of the feature. In comparison, the init attribute can be written out without any complications.

Anonymous Functions in Python

Anonymous functions are often termed lambda functions in Python since you are using the lambda keyword rather than naming it with the standard-def keyword.

1.   double = lambda x: x*2

2.   double(5)

The anonymous or lambda feature in the DataCamp Light chunk above is lambda x: x*2. X is the argument, and x*2 is the interpretation or instruction that is analyzed and given back. What is unique about this function, and it has no tag, like the examples you saw in the first section of the lecture for this function. When you had to write the above function in a UDF, you would get the following result:

def double(x):

return x*2

Let us see another example of a lambda function where two arguments are used:

1. # `sum()` lambda function

2.   sum = lambda x, y: x + y;

3. # Call the `sum()` anonymous function

4.   sum(4,5)

5. # "Translate" to a UDF

6.   def sum(x, y):

7. returnx+y

When you need a function with no name for a short interval of time, you utilize anonymous functions and this is generated at runtime. Special contexts where this is important are when operating with filter(), map() and redu():

1. from functools import reduce

2. my_list = [1,2,3,4,5,6,7,8,9,10]

3. # Use lambda function with `filter()`

4. filtered_list = list(filter(lambda x: (x*2 > 10), my_list))

5. # Use lambda function with `map()`

6. mapped_list = list(map(lambda x: x*2, my_list))

7. # Use lambda function with `reduce()`

8. reduced_list = reduce(lambda x, y: x+y, my_list)

9. print(filtered_list)

10. print(mapped_list)

11. print(reduced_list)

As the name states the filter() function it help filters the original list of inputs my_list based on a criterion > 10.By contrast, with map(), you implement a function to every components in the my_listlist. You multiply all of the components with two in this scenario. Remember that the function reduce() is a portion of the functools library. You cumulatively are using this function to the components in the my_list() list, from left to right, and in this situation decrease the sequence to a single value 55.

Using main() as a Function

If you have got any knowledge with other programming languages like java, you'll notice that executing functions requires the main feature. As you've known in the above examples, Python doesn't really require this. However, it can be helpful to logically organize your code along with a main() function in your python code- - all of the most important components are contained within this main() function.

You could even simply achieve and call a main() function the same as you did with all of those above functions:

1. # Define `main()` function

2. def main():

3. hello()

4. print("This is the main function")

5. main()

After all, as it now appears, when you load it as a module, the script of your main ( ) function will indeed be called. You invoke the main() function whenever name == ' main ' to ensure this does not happen.

That implies the source above code script becomes:

1.# Define `main()` function

2.def main():

3.hello()

4.print("This is a main function")

5.# Execute `main()` function

6. if__name__ == '__main__':

7. main()

Remember that in addition to the main function, you too have a init function, which validates a class or object instance. Plainly defined, it operates as a constructor or initializer, and is termed automatically when you start a new class instance. With such a function, the freshly formed object is assigned to the self-parameter that you've seen in this guide earlier.

Consider the following example:

class Dog:

"""

Requires:

legs – legs for a dog to walk.

color – Fur color.

"""

def __init__(self, legs, color):

self.legs = legs

self.color = color

def bark(self):

bark = "bark" * 2

return bark

```python
if __name__ == "__main__":

dog = Dog(4, "brown")

bark = dog.bark()

print(bark)
```

LISTS AND LOOPS

Lists

Alist is often a data structure in Python, which is an ordered list of elements that is mutable or modifiable. An item is named for each element or value inside a list. Just like strings are defined like characters between quotations, lists are specified by square brackets '[ ]' having values.

Lists are nice to have because you have other similar principles to deal with. They help you to hold data that are relevant intact, compress the code, and run the same numerous-value methods and processes at once.

It could be helpful to get all the several lists you have on your computer when beginning to think about Python lists as well as other data structures that are types of collections: Your assemblage of files, song playlists, browser bookmarks, emails, video collections that you can access through a streaming platform and much more.

We must function with this data table, taken from data collection of the Mobile App Store (RamanathanPerumal):

Name	price	currency	rating_count	rating
Instagram	0.0	USD	2161558	4.5
Clash of Clans	0.0	USD	2130805	4.5

Temple Run	0.0	USD	1724546	4.5
Pandora — Music & Radio	0.0	USD	1126879	4.0
Facebook	0.0	USD	2974676	3.5

Every value is a data point in the table. The first row (just after titles of the columns) for example has 5 data points:

- Facebook
- 0.0
- USD
- 2974676
- 3.5

Dataset consists of a collection of data points. We can consider the above table as a list of data points. Therefore we consider the entire list a dataset. We can see there are five rows and five columns to our data set.

Utilizing our insight of the Python types, we could perhaps consider we can store each data point in their own variable — for example, here's how we can store the data points of the first row:

```
script.py
track_name_row1 = 'Facebook'
price_row1 = 0.0
currency_row1 = 'USD'
rating_count_tot_row1 = 2974676
user_rating_row1 = 3.5
```

Above, we stored:

- Text for the string as "Facebook."
- Float 0.0 as a price
- Text for the string as "USD."
- Integer 2,974,676 as a rating count
- Float 3.5 for user rating

A complicated process would be to create a variable for every data point in our data set. Luckily we can use lists to store data more effectively. So in the first row, we can draw up a list of data points:

```
script.py

row_1 = ['Facebook', 0.0, 'USD', 2974676, 3.5]
print(row_1)
type(row_1)
```

```
Output
['Facebook', 0.0, 'USD', 2974676, 3.5]
list
```

For list creation, we:

- Separating each with a comma while typing out a sequence of data points: 'Facebook,' 0.0, 'USD,' 2974676, 3.5
- Closing the list with square brackets: ['Facebook', 0.0, 'USD', 2974676, 3.5]
- After the list is created, we assign it to a variable named row_1and the list is stored in the computer's memory.

For creating data points list, we only need to:

- Add comma to the data points for separation.
- Closing the list with brackets.

See below as we create five lists, in the dataset each row with one list:

```
row_1 =]['FACEBOOK', 0.0, 'usd', 2974676, 3.5]

row_2 = ['INSTAGRAM', 0.0, 'usd', 2161558, 4.5

row_3 = ['CLASH OF CLANS', 0.0, 'usd', 2130805, 4.5]

row_4 = ['TEMPLE RUN', 0.0, 'usd', 1724546, 4.5]

row_5 =['PANDORA', 0.0, 'usd', 1126879, 4.0]
```

Index of Python Lists

A list could include a broader array of data types. A list containing [4, 5, 6] includes the same types of data (only integers), while the list ['Facebook', 0.0, 'USD,' 2974676, 3.5] contains many types of data:

- Consisting Two types of floats (0.0, 3.5)
- Consisting One type of integer (2974676)
- Consisting two types of strings ('Facebook,' 'USD')

`['FACEBOOK', 0.0, 'usd', 2974676, 3.5]` list got 5 data points. For the length of a list, len() command can be used:

```
script.py
row_1 = ['Facebook', 0.0, 'USD', 2974676, 3.5]
print(len(row_1))

list_1 = [1, 6, 0]
print(len(list_1))

list_2 = []
print(len(list_2))

Output
5
3
0
```

For smaller lists, we can simply count the data points on our displays to figure the length, but perhaps the len() command will claim to be very useful anytime you function with lists containing many components, or just need to compose data code where you really don't know the length in advance.

Every other component (data point) in a list is linked to a particular number, termed the index number. The indexing also begins at 0, which means that the first element should have the index number 0, the 2nd element the index number 1, etc.

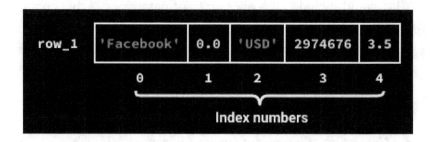

To locate a list element index rapidly, determine its location number in the list and then subtract it by 1. The string 'USD,' for instance, is the third item in the list (stance number 3), well its index number must be two because $3 - 1 = 2$.

The index numbers enable us to locate a single item from a list. Going backward through the list row 1 from the example above, by executing code row 1[0], we can obtain the first node (the string 'Facebook') of index number 0.

```
script.py

row_1 = ['Facebook', 0.0, 'USD', 2974676, 3.5]
row_1[0]
```

```
Output
'Facebook'
```

The Model list_name[index number] follows the syntax for locating specific list components. For example, the title of our list above is row_1 and the index number of a first element is 0, we get row_1[0] continuing to follow the list_name[index number] model, in which the index number 0 is in square brackets just after the name of the variable row_1.

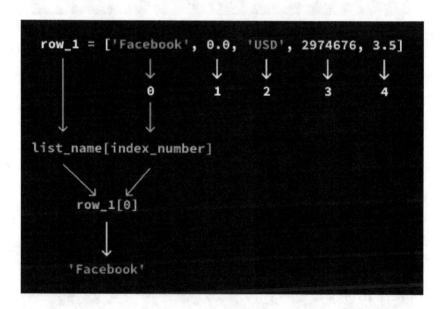

The method to retrieve each element in row_1:

```
script.py

row_1 = ['Facebook', 0.0, 'USD', 2974676, 3.5]
            0          1      2      3        4
            └──────────────┬──────────────────┘
                    Index numbers

print(row_1[0])
print(row_1[1])
print(row_1[2])
print(row_1[3])
print(row_1[4])
```
```
Output
Facebook
0.0
USD
2974676
3.5
```

Retrieval of list elements makes processes easier to execute. For example, Facebook and Instagram ratings can be selected, and the aggregate or distinction between the two can be found:

```
script.py

row_1 = ['Facebook', 0.0, 'USD', 2974676, 3.5]
row_2 = ['Instagram', 0.0, 'USD', 2161558, 4.5]

difference = row_2[4] - row_1[4]
average_rating = (row_1[4] + row_2[4]) / 2

print(difference)
print(average_rating)
```
```
Output
1.0
4.0
```

Try Using list indexing to retrieve and then average the number of ratings with the first 3 rows:

ratings_1 = row_1[3]

ratings_2 = row_2[3]

ratings_3 = row_3[3]

total = ratings_1 + ratings_2 + ratings_3

average = total / 3

print(average)

2422346.3333333335

Using Negative Indexing with Lists

There are two indexing systems for lists in Python:

1. Positive indexing: The index number of the first element is 0; the index number of the second element is 1 and furthermore.
2. Negative indexing: The index number of the last element is -1; the index number of the second element is -2 and furthermore.

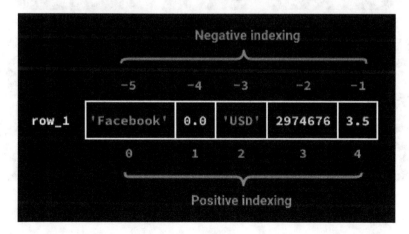

In exercise, we mostly use positive indexing to obtain elements of the list. Negative indexing is helpful whenever we want to pick the last element in such a list, mostly if the list is lengthy, and by calculating, we cannot figure out the length.

```
script.py
row_1 = ['Facebook', 0.0, 'USD', 2974676, 3.5]

print(row_1[-1])
print(row_1[4])

Output
3.5
3.5
```

Note that when we use an index number just outside of the scope of the two indexing schemes, we are going to have an IndexError.

```
script.py
row_1 = ['Facebook', 0.0, 'USD', 2974676, 3.5]
row_1[6]

Output
IndexError: list index out of range
```

```
script.py
row_1 = ['Facebook', 0.0, 'USD', 2974676, 3.5]
row_1[-7]

Output
IndexError: list index out of range
```

How about using negative indexing to remove from each of the top 3 rows the user rating (the very last value) and afterwards average it.

row_1 [-1]=rating_1

row_2[-1]=rating_2

row_3[-1]=rating_3

rating_1 + rating_2 + rating_3=total_rating

total_rating / 3= average_rating

print(average)

2422346.33333

Slice Python Lists

Rather than selecting the list elements separately, we can pick two consecutive elements using a syntax shortcut:

```
script.py
row_3 = ['Clash of Clans', 0.0, 'USD', 2130805, 4.5]

cc_pricing_data = row_3[0:3]  ⟵ syntax shortcut
print(cc_pricing_data)

Output
['Clash of Clans', 0.0, 'USD']
```

While selecting the first n elements from a list called a list (n stands for a number), we can use the list syntax shortcut [0: n]. In the above example, we had to choose from the list row 3 the first three elements, so we will use row 3[0:3].

When the first three items were chosen, we sliced a portion of the set. For this function, the collection method for a section of a list is known as list slicing.

List slice can be done in many ways:

Retrieving any list slice we need:

- Firstly identify the first and last elements of the slice.
- The index numbers of the first and last element of the slice must then be defined.
- Lastly, we can use the syntax a list[m: n] to extract the list slice we require, while:

'm' means the index number of both the slice's 1st element; and 'n' symbolizes the index number of the slice's last element in addition to one (if the last element seems to have index number 2, after which n is 3, if the last element seems to have index number 4, after which n is 5, and so on).

The slice we want

```
row_3 = ['Clash of Clans', 0.0, 'USD', 2130805, 4.5]
```

(Step 1) Identify the first and the last element of the slice: `0.0` is the first element, and `2130805` is the last.

(Step 2) Identify the index numbers of the first and the last element of the slice: `0.0` has the index number 1, and `2130805` has the index number 3.

(Step 3) Retrieve the list slice by using `a_list[m:n]`: `row_3[1:4]` — remember that n is the index number of the last element plus one (3 + 1, in this case)

When we want to choose the 1st or last 'x' elements (x represents a number), we may use even less complex shortcuts for syntax:

a_list[:x] when we need to choose the first x elements.

a_list[-x:] when we need to choose the last x elements.

```
script.py

row_3 = ['Clash of Clans', 0.0, 'USD', 2130805, 4.5]

first_3 = row_3[:3]
last_3 = row_3[-3:]

print(first_3)
print(last_3)
```

```
Output
['Clash of Clans', 0.0, 'USD']
['USD', 2130805, 4.5]
```

See how we retrieve from the first row the first four elements (with Facebook data):

first_4_fb = row_1[:4]

print(first_4_fb)

['Facebook', 0.0, 'USD', 2974676]

From the same row, the last three elements are:

last_3_fb = row_1[-3:]

print(last_3_fb)

['USD', 2974676, 3.5]

In the fifth row (data in the row for Pandora) with elements third and fourth are:

pandora_3_4 = row_5[2:4]

```
print(pandora_3_4)
```

```
['USD', 1126879]
```

Python List of Lists

Lists were previously introduced as a viable approach to using one variable per data point. Rather than having a different variable for any of the five 'Facebook' data points, 0.0, 'USD,' 2974676, 3.5, we can connect the data points into a list together and then save the list in a variable.

We have worked with a data set of five rows since then and have stored each row as a collection in each different variable (row 1, row 2, row 3, row 4, and row 5 variables). Even so, if we had a data set of 5,000 rows, we would probably have ended up with 5,000 variables that will create our code messy and nearly difficult to work with.

To fix this issue, we may store our five variables in a unified list:

```
script.py
row_1 = ['Facebook', 0.0, 'USD', 2974676, 3.5]
row_2 = ['Instagram', 0.0, 'USD', 2161558, 4.5]
row_3 = ['Clash of Clans', 0.0, 'USD', 2130805, 4.5]
row_4 = ['Temple Run', 0.0, 'USD', 1724546, 4.5]
row_5 = ['Pandora - Music & Radio', 0.0, 'USD', 1126879, 4.0]

data_set = [row_1, row_2, row_3, row_4, row_5]
data_set
```

```
Output         Notice the double brackets

[['Facebook', 0.0, 'USD', 2974676, 3.5],        Notice the commas
['Instagram', 0.0, 'USD', 2161558, 4.5],
['Clash of Clans', 0.0, 'USD', 2130805, 4.5],
['Temple Run', 0.0, 'USD', 1724546, 4.5],
['Pandora - Music & Radio', 0.0, 'USD', 1126879, 4.0]]
```

As we're seeing, the data set is a list of five additional columns (row 1, row 2, row 3, row 4, and row 5). A list containing other lists is termed a set of lists.

The data set variable is already a list, which indicates that we can use the syntax we have learned to retrieve individual list elements and execute list slicing. Under, we have:

- Use datset[0] to locate the first list element (row 1).
- Use datset[-1] to locate the last list element (row 5).
- Obtain the first two list elements (row 1 and row 2) utilizing data set[:2] to execute a list slicing.

```
script.py
data_set = [row_1, row_2, row_3, row_4, row_5]
print(data_set[0])
print(data_set[-1])
print(data_set[:2])

Output
['Facebook', 0.0, 'USD', 2974676, 3.5]
['Pandora - Music & Radio', 0.0, 'USD', 1126879, 4.0]
[['Facebook', 0.0, 'USD', 2974676, 3.5],
['Instagram', 0.0, 'USD', 2161558, 4.5]]
```

Often, we will need to obtain individual elements from a list that is a portion of a list of lists — for example; we might need to obtain the rating of 3.5 from the data row ['FACEBOOK', 0.0, 'USD', 2974676, 3.5], which is a portion of the list of data sets. We retrieve 3.5 from data set below utilizing what we have learnt:

- Using data set[0], we locate row_1, and allocate the output to a variable named fb_row.

- fb_row ['Facebook', 0.0, 'USD', 2974676, 3.5] outputs, which we printed.
- Using fb_row[-1], we locate the final element from fb_row (because fb row is a list), and appoint the output to a variable called fb_rating.
- Print fb_rating, outputting 3.5

```
script.py
data_set = [row_1, row_2, row_3, row_4, row_5]
fb_row = data_set[0]
print(fb_row)

fb_rating = fb_row[-1]
print(fb_rating)

Output
['Facebook', 0.0, 'USD', 2974676, 3.5]
3.5
```

Earlier in this example, we obtained 3.5 in two steps: data_set[0] was first retrieved, and fb_row[-1] was then retrieved. There is also an easy way to get the same 3.5 output by attaching the two indices ([0] and [-1]); the code data_set[0][-1] gets 3.5.:

```
script.py
data_set = [row_1, row_2, row_3, row_4, row_5]
print(data_set[0][-1])
            ⎵⎵⎵⎵⎵⎵⎵
              row_1
              ⎵⎵⎵
   ['Facebook', 0.0, 'USD', 2974676, 3.5]

Output
3.5
```

Earlier in this example, we have seen two ways to get the 3.5 value back. Both methods lead to the same performance (3.5), but the second approach requires fewer coding, as the steps we see from the example are elegantly integrated. As you can select an alternative, people generally prefer the latter.

Let's turn our five independent lists in to the list of lists:

app_data_set = [row_1, row_2, row_3, row_4, row_5]

then use:

print(app_data_set)

```
[

 ['FACEBOOK', 0.0, 'usd', 2974676, 3.5]

 ['INSTAGRAM', 0.0, 'usd', 2161558, 4.5

 ['CLASH OF CLANS', 0.0, 'usd', 2130805, 4.5]

 ['TEMPLE RUN', 0.0, 'usd', 1724546, 4.5]

 ['PANDORA', 0.0, 'usd', 1126879, 4.0]                    ]
```

List Processes by Repetitive method

Earlier, we had an interest in measuring an app's average ranking in this project. It was a feasible task while we were attempting to work only for three rows, but the tougher it becomes, the further rows we add. Utilizing our tactic from the beginning, we will:

1. Obtain each individual rating.
2. Take the sum of the ratings.
3. Dividing by the total number of ratings.

```
script.py

row_1 = ['Facebook', 0.0, 'USD', 2974676, 3.5]
row_2 = ['Instagram', 0.0, 'USD', 2161558, 4.5]
row_3 = ['Clash of Clans', 0.0, 'USD', 2130805, 4.5]
row_4 = ['Temple Run', 0.0, 'USD', 1724546, 4.5]
row_5 = ['Pandora - Music & Radio', 0.0, 'USD', 1126879, 4.0]

app_data_set = [row_1, row_2, row_3, row_4, row_5]
avg_rating = (app_data_set[0][-1] + app_data_set[1][-1] +
              app_data_set[2][-1] + app_data_set[3][-1] +
              app_data_set[4][-1]) / 5

avg_rating
```

```
Output
4.2
```

As you have seen that it becomes complicated with five ratings. Unless we were dealing with data that includes thousands of rows, an unimaginable amount of code would be needed! We ought to find a quick way to get lots of ratings back.

Taking a look at the code example earlier in this thread, we see that a procedure continues to reiterate: within app_data_set, we select the last list element for every list. What if we can just directly ask Python we would like to repeat this process in app_data_set for every list?

Luckily we can use it — Python gives us a simple route to repeat a plan that helps us tremendously when we have to reiterate a process tens of thousands or even millions of times.

Let's assume we have a list [3, 5, 1, 2] allocated to a variable rating, and we need to replicate the following procedure: display the element for each element in the ratings. And this is how we can turn it into syntax with Python:

```
script.py

ratings = [3, 5, 1, 2]

for element in ratings:
    print(element)
```

```
Output

3
5
1
2
```

The procedure that we decided to replicate in our first example above was "generate the last item for each list in the app_data_set." Here's how we can transform that operation into syntax with Python:

```
script.py

app_data_set = [row_1, row_2, row_3, row_4, row_5]

for each_list in app_data_set:
    rating = each_list[-1]
    print(rating)
```

```
Output

3.5
4.5
4.5
4.5
4.0
```

Let's attempt and then get a good idea of what's going on above. Python differentiates each list item from app_data_set, each at a time, and assign it to each_list (which essentially becomes a vector that holds a list — we'll address this further):

```
script.py

app_data_set = [row_1, row_2, row_3, row_4, row_5]

for each_list in app_data_set:
    print(each_list)

Output

['Facebook', 0.0, 'USD', 2974676, 3.5]
['Instagram', 0.0, 'USD', 2161558, 4.5]
['Clash of Clans', 0.0, 'USD', 2130805, 4.5]
['Temple Run', 0.0, 'USD', 1724546, 4.5]
['Pandora - Music & Radio', 0.0, 'USD', 1126879, 4.0]
```

In the last figure earlier in this thread, the code is a much simpler and much more conceptual edition of the code below:

```
script.py

app_data_set = [row_1, row_2, row_3, row_4, row_5]

print(app_data_set[0])
print(app_data_set[1])
print(app_data_set[2])          for each_list in app_data_set:
print(app_data_set[3])              print(each_list)
print(app_data_set[4])

Output

['Facebook', 0.0, 'USD', 2974676, 3.5]
['Instagram', 0.0, 'USD', 2161558, 4.5]
['Clash of Clans', 0.0, 'USD', 2130805, 4.5]
['Temple Run', 0.0, 'USD', 1724546, 4.5]
['Pandora - Music & Radio', 0.0, 'USD', 1126879, 4.0]
```

Utilizing the above technique requires that we consider writing a line of code for each row in the data set. But by using the app_data_set methodology for each list involves that we write only two lines of code irrespective of the number of rows in the data set — the data set may have five rows or a hundred thousand.

Our transitional goal is to use this special method to calculate the average rating of our five rows above, in which our ultimate goal is to calculate the average rating of 7,197 rows for our data set. We 're going to get exactly that within the next few displays of this task, but we're going to concentrate for now on practicing this method to get a strong grasp of it.

We ought to indent the space characters four times to the right before we want to write the code:

```
script.py

app_data_set = [row_1, row_2, row_3, row_4, row_5]

for each_list in app_data_set:
    print(each_list)
```

We need to indent the code we want repeated
four space characters to the right

Theoretically, we would only have to indent the code to the right with at least one space character, but in the Python language, the declaration is to use four space characters. This assists with readability — reading your code will be fairly easy for other individuals who watch this convention, and you will find it easier to follow theirs.

Now use this technique to print each app's name and rating:

foreach_list in app_data_set:

name = each_list[0]

rating = each_list[-1]

print(name, rating)

Facebook 3.5

Instagram 4.5

Clash of Clans 4.5

Temple Run 4.5

Pandora - Music & Radio 4.0

Loops

A loop is frequently used to iterate over a series of statements. We have two kinds of loops, 'for loop' and 'while loop' in Python. We will study 'for loop' and 'while loop' in the following scenario.

For Loop

Python's for loop is used to iterate over a sequence (list, tuple, string) or just about any iterate-able object. It is called traversal to iterate over a sequence.

Syntax of For loop in Python

for<variable> in <sequence>:

  # body_of_loop that has set of statements

  # which requires repeated execution

In this case < variable > is often a variable used to iterate over a < sequence >. Around each iteration the next value is taken from < sequence > to approach the end of the sequence.

Python – For loop example

The example below illustrates the use of a loop to iterate over a list array. We calculate the square of each number present in the list and show the same with the body of for loop.

```
#Printing squares of all numbers program

# List of integer numbers

numbers = [1, 2, 4, 6, 11, 20]

#variable to store each number's square temporary

sq = 0

#iterating over the given list

forval in numbers:

    # calculating square of each number

sq = val * val

    # displaying the squares

print(sq)
```

Output:

1

4

16

36

121

400

For loop with else block

Excluding Java, we can have the loop linked with an optional 'else' block in Python. The 'else' block only runs after all the iterations are finished by the loop. Let's see one example:

For val in range(5):

    print(val)

else:

    print("The loop has completed execution")

Output:

0

1

2

3

4

The loop has completed execution

Note: else block is executed when the loop is completed.

Nested For loop in Python

If there is a loop within another for loop, then it will be termed a nested for loop. Let's take a nested for loop example.

```python
for num1 in range(3):

    for num2 in range(10, 14):

        print(num1, ",", num2)
```

Output:

0 , 10

0 , 11

0 , 12

0 , 13

1 , 10

1 , 11

1 , 12

1 , 13

2 , 10

2 , 11

2 , 12

2 , 13

While Loop

While loop is also used to continuously iterate over a block of code until a specified statement returns false, we have seen in many for loop in Python in the last guide, which is used for a similar intent. The biggest distinction is that we use for looping when we are not sure how many times the loop needs execution, yet on the other side when we realize exactly how many times we have to execute the loop, we need for a loop.

Syntax of while loop

while conditioning:

    #body_of_while

The body of the while is a series of statements from Python which require repetitive implementation. These claims are consistently executed until the specified condition returns false.

while loop flow

1. Firstly given condition is inspected, the loop is canceled if the condition returns false, and also the control moves towards the next statement in the compiler after the loop.

2. When the condition returns true, the set of statements within the loop will be performed, and the power will then switch to the loop start for the next execution.

Those two measures continuously occur as long as the condition defined in the loop stands true.

While loop example

This is an example of a while loop. We have a variable number in this case, and we show the value of the number in a loop, the loop will have an incremental operation where we increase the number value. It is a very crucial component, while the loop should have an operation of increase or decrease. Otherwise, the loop will operate indefinitely.

```
num = 1

#loop will repeat itself as long as it can

#num< 10 remains true

whilenum< 10:`

print(num)

    #incrementing the value of num

num = num + 3
```

Output:

1

4

7

Infinite while loop

Example 1:

This will endlessly print the word 'hello' since this situation will always be true.

```
while True:

print("hello")
```

Example 2:

```
num = 1

whilenum<5:

print(num)
```

This will endlessly print '1' since we do not update the number value inside the loop, so the number value would always remain one, and the condition number<5 would always give back true.

Nested while loop in Python

While inside another while loop a while loop is present, then it will be considered nested while loop. To understand this concept, let us take an example.

```
i = 1

j = 5

while i< 4:

while j < 8:

print(i, ",", j)

     j = j + 1

i = i + 1
```

Output:

1 , 5

2 , 6

3 , 7

Python – while loop with else block

We may add an 'else' block to a while loop. The section 'else' is possible. It executes only when the processing of the loop has ended.

num = 10

whilenum> 6:

print(num)

num = num-1

else:

print("loop is finished")

Output:

10

9

8

7

Loop is finished

ADDING MULTIPLE VALUED DATA IN PYTHON

O ften the creator wants users to input multiple values or inputs in a line. In Python, users could use two techniques to take multiple values or inputs in one line.

1. Use of split() method
2. Use of List comprehension

Use of split() method :

This feature helps to receive many user inputs. It splits the defined separator to the given input. If no separator is given, then a separator is blank space. Users generally use a split() method to separate a Python string, but it can be used when multiple inputs are taken.

Syntax:

input().split(separator, maxsplit)

Example:

```
filter_none
edit
play_arrow
brightness_4
#Python program showing how to add
#multiple input using split
#taking two inputs each time
x, y = input("Enter a two value: ").split()
print("Number of boys: ", x)
print("Number of girls: ", y)
print()
# taking three inputs at a time
x, y, z = input("Enter a three value: ").split()
print("Total number of students: ", x)
print("Number of boys is : ", y)
print("Number of girls is : ", z)
print()
# taking two inputs at a time
a, b = input("Enter a two value: ").split()
print("First number is {} and second number is {}".format(a, b))
print()
# taking multiple inputs at a time
# and type casting using list() function
x = list(map(int, input("Enter a multiple value: ").split()))
print("List of students: ", x)
```

Output:

```
Enter a two value: 5 10
Number of boys:  5
Number of girls:  10

Enter a three value: 30 10 20
Total number of students:  30
Number of boys is :  10
Number of girls is :  20

Enter a four value: 20 30
First number is 20 and second number is 30

Enter a multiple value: 20 30 10 22 23 26
List of students:  [20, 30, 10, 22, 23, 26]
```

Using List comprehension:

Comprehension of lists is an easy way of describing and building a list in Python. Just like mathematical statements, we can generate lists within each line only. It is often used when collecting multiple device inputs.

Example:

```
filter_none
edit
play_arrow
brightness_4
# Python program showing
# how to take multiple input
# using List comprehension
# taking two input at a time
x, y = [int(x) for x in input("Enter two value: ").split()]
print("First Number is: ", x)
print("Second Number is: ", y)
print()
# taking three input at a time
x, y, z = [int(x) for x in input("Enter three value: ").split()]
print("First Number is: ", x)
print("Second Number is: ", y)
print("Third Number is: ", z)
print()
# taking two inputs at a time
x, y = [int(x) for x in input("Enter two value: ").split()]
print("First number is {} and second number is {}".format(x, y))
print()
# taking multiple inputs at a time
x = [int(x) for x in input("Enter multiple value: ").split()]
print("Number of list is: ", x)
```

Output:

```
Enter two value: 2 5
First Number is:   2
Second Number is:   5

Enter three value: 2 4 5
First Number is:   2
Second Number is:   4
Third Number is:   5

Enter two value: 2 10
First number is 2 and second number is 10

Enter multiple value: 1 2 3 4 5
Number of list is:   [1, 2, 3, 4, 5]
```

Note: The definitions above take inputs divided by spaces. If we prefer to pursue different input by comma (","), we can just use the below:

taking multiple inputs divided by comma at a time

x = [int(x) for x in input("Enter multiple value: ").split(",")]

print("Number of list is: ", x)

Assign multiple values to multiple variables

By separating the variables and values with commas, you can allocate multiple values to different variables.

a, b = 100, 200

print(a)

100

print(b)

200

You have more than three variables to delegate. In addition, various types can be assigned, as well.

a, b, c = 0.1, 100, 'string'

print(a)

0.1

print(b)

100

print(c)

#string

Assign the same value to multiple variables

Using = consecutively, you could even appoint multiple variables with the same value. For instance, this is helpful when you initialize multiple variables to almost the same value.

a = b = 100

print(a)

100

print(b)

100

Upon defining the same value, another value may also be converted into one. As explained later, when allocating mutable objects such as lists or dictionaries, care should be taken.

a = 200

print(a)

200

print(b)

100

It can be written three or more in the same way.

a = b = c = 'string'

print(a)

string

print(b)

string

print(c)

string

Instead of immutable objects like int, float, and str, be careful when appointing mutable objects like list and dict.

When you use = consecutively, all variables are assigned the same object, so if you modify the element value or create a new element, then the other object will also modify.

```
a = b = [0, 1, 2]

print(a is b)

# True

a[0] = 100

print(a)

# [100, 1, 2]

print(b)

# [100, 1, 2]
```

Same as below.

```
b = [0, 1, 2]

a = b

print(a is b)

# True

a[0] = 100

print(a)

# [100, 1, 2]
```

```
print(b)
```

```
# [100, 1, 2]
```

If you would like to independently manage them you need to allocate them separately.

after c = []; d = [], c and d are guaranteed to link to two unique, newly created empty,different lists. (Note that c = d = [] assigns the same object to both c and d.)

Here is another example:

```
a = [0, 1, 2]
```

```
b = [0, 1, 2]
```

```
print(a is b)
```

```
# False
```

```
a[0] = 100
```

```
print(a)
```

```
# [100, 1, 2]
```

```
print(b)
```

```
# [0, 1, 2]
```

ADDING STRING DATA IN PYTHON

What is String in Python?

A string is a Character set. A character is just a symbol. The English language, for instance, has 26 characters. Operating systems do not handle characters they handle the (binary) numbers. And if you may see characters on your computer, it is represented internally as a mixture of 0s and 1s and is manipulated. The transformation of character to a number is known as encoding, and probably decoding is the reverse process. ASCII and Unicode are two of the widely used encodings. A string in Python is a series of characters in Unicode. Unicode was incorporated to provide all characters in all languages and to carry encoding uniformity. Python Unicode allows you to learn regarding Unicode.

How to create a string in Python?

Strings may be formed by encapsulating characters or even double quotes inside a single quotation. In Python, even triple quotes may be used but commonly used to portray multiline strings and docstrings.

```
# defining strings in Python

# all of the following are equivalent

my_string = 'Hello'

print(my_string)

my_string = "Hello"

print(my_string)

my_string = '''Hello'''

print(my_string)

# triple quotes string can extend multiple lines

my_string = """Hello, welcome to the world of Python"""

print(my_string)
```

When the program is executed, the output becomes:

```
Hello

Hello

Hello

Hello, welcome to the world of Python
```

Accessing the characters in a string?

By indexing and using slicing, we can obtain individual characters and scope of characters. The index commences at 0. Attempting to obtain a character from index range will cause an IndexError to increase. The index has to be integral. We cannot use floats or other types, and this will lead to TypeError. Python lets its sequences be indexed negatively. The -1 index corresponds to the last object, -2 to the second object, and so forth. Using the slicing operator '(colon),' we can access a range of items within a string.

#Python string characters access:

```
str = 'programiz'
print('str = ', str)
#first character
print('str[0] = ', str[0])
#last character
print('str[-1] = ', str[-1])
#slicing 2nd to 5th character
print('str[1:5] = ', str[1:5])
#slicing 6th to 2nd last character
print('str[5:-2] = ', str[5:-2])
If we execute the code above we have the following results:
str =   programiz
str[0] =   p
str[-1] =   z
str[1:5] =   rogr
str[5:-2] =   am
```

When we attempt to access an index out of the range, or if we are using numbers other than an integer, errors will arise.

index must be in the range

```
>>>my_string[15]
```

...

```
IndexError: string index out of range
```

```
# index must be an integer
```

```
>>>my_string[1.5]
```

...

TypeError: Define string indices as integers only

By analyzing the index between the elements as seen below, slicing can best be visualized. Whenever we want to obtain a range, we need the index that slices the part of the string from it.

How to change or delete a string?

Strings are unchangeable. This means elements of a list cannot be modified until allocated. We will easily reassign various strings of the same term.

```
>>>my_string = 'programiz'
```

```
>>>my_string[5] = 'a'
```

...

```
TypeError: 'str' object does not support item assignment
```

```
>>>my_string = 'Python'
```

```
>>>my_string
```

```
'Python'
```

We cannot erase characters from a string, or remove them. But it's easy to erase the string completely by using del keyword.

```
>>>delmy_string[1]

...

TypeError: 'str' object doesn't support item deletion

>>>delmy_string

>>>my_string

...

NameError: name 'my_string' is not defined
```

Python String Operations

There are many methods that can be used with string making it one of the most commonly used Python data types. See Python Data Types for more information on the types of data used in Python coding

Concatenation of Two or More Strings

The combination of two or even more strings into one is termed concatenation. In Python, the + operator does that. They are likewise concatenated by actually typing two string literals together. For a specified number of times, the * operator could be used to reiterate the string.

```
# Python String Operations

str1 = 'Hello'

str2 ='World!'

# using +

print('str1 + str2 = ', str1 + str2)

# using *

print('str1 * 3 =', str1 * 3)
```

Once we execute the program above we get the following results:

```
str1 + str2 =  HelloWorld!

str1 * 3 = HelloHelloHello
```

Using two literal strings together would therefore concatenate them like + operator.

We might use parentheses if we wish to concatenate strings in various lines.
```
>>> # two string literals together

>>> 'Hello ''World!'

'Hello World!'

>>> # using parentheses

>>> s = ('Hello '

...      'World')

>>>s

'Hello World'
```

Iterating Through a string

With a for loop, we can iterate through a string. This is an example of counting the number of 'l's in a string function.

```
#Iterating through a string

count = 0

for letter in 'Hello World':

if(letter == 'l'):

count += 1

print(count,'letters found')
```

If we execute the code above, we have the following results:

'3 letters found.'

String Membership Test

We can check whether or not there is a substring within a string by using keyword in.

>>> 'a' in 'program'

True

>>> 'at' not in 'battle'

False

Built-in functions to Work with Python

Different built-in functions which can also be work with strings in series. A few other commonly used types are len() and enumerate(). The function enumerate() returns an enumerate object. It includes the index and value as combinations of all elements in the string. This may be of use to iteration. Comparably, len() returns the string length (characters number).

```
str = 'cold'

# enumerate()

list_enumerate = list(enumerate(str))

print('list(enumerate(str) = ', list_enumerate)

#character count

print('len(str) = ', len(str))
```

Once we execute the code above we have the following results:

```
list(enumerate(str) =  [(0, 'c'), (1, 'o'), (2, 'l'), (3, 'd')]

len(str) =  4
```

Formats for Python String

Sequence for escaping

We can't use single quotes or double quotes if we want to print a text like He said, "What's there?" This would result in a SyntaxError because there are single and double quotations in the text alone.

>>>print("He said, "What's there?"")

...

SyntaxError: invalid syntax

>>>print('He said, "What's there?"')

...

SyntaxError: invalid syntax

Triple quotes are one way to get round the problem. We might use escape sequences as a solution. A series of escape starts with a backslash, which is represented differently. If we are using a single quote to describe a string, it is important to escape all single quotes within the string. The case with double quotes is closely related. This is how the above text can be represented.

```
# using triple quotes

print('''He said, "What's there?"''')

# escaping single quotes

print('He said, "What\'s there?"')

# escaping double quotes

print("He said, \"What's there?\"")
```

Once we execute the code above, we have the following results:

He said, "What's there?"

He said, "What's there?"

He said, "What's there?"

Raw String to ignore escape sequence

Quite often inside a string, we might want to reject the escape sequences. To use it, we can set r or R before the string. Which means it's a raw string, and it will neglect any escape sequence inside.

>>>print("This is \x61 \ngood example")

This is a

good example

>>> print(r"This is \x61 \ngood example")

This is \x61 \ngood example

The format() Method for Formatting Strings

The format() sources available and make with the string object is very flexible and potent in string formatting. Style strings contain curly braces{} as placeholders or fields of substitution, which are substituted.

To specify the sequence, we may use positional arguments or keyword arguments.

```
# Python string format() method
# default(implicit) order
default_order = "{}, {} and {}".format('John','Bill','Sean')
print('\n--- Default Order ---')
print(default_order)
# order using positional argument
positional_order = "{1}, {0} and {2}".format('John','Bill','Sean')
print('\n--- Positional Order ---')
print(positional_order)
# order using keyword argument
keyword_order = "{s}, {b} and {j}".format(j='John',b='Bill',s='Sean')
print('\n--- Keyword Order ---')
print(keyword_order)
Once we execute the code above we have the following results:
--- Default Order ---
John, Bill and Sean
--- Positional Order ---
Bill, John and Sean
--- Keyword Order ---
Sean, Bill and John
```

The format() technique can have requirements in optional format. Using colon, they are divided from the name of the field. For example, a string in the given space may be left-justified <, right-justified >, or based ^.

Even we can format integers as binary, hexadecimal, etc. and floats can be rounded or shown in the style of the exponent. You can use tons of compiling there. For all string formatting available using the format() method, see below example:

```
>>> # formatting integers
>>> "Binary representation of {0} is {0:b}".format(12)
'Binary representation of 12 is 1100'
>>> # formatting floats
>>> "Exponent representation: {0:e}".format(1566.345)
'Exponent representation: 1.566345e+03'
>>> # round off
>>> "One third is: {0:.3f}".format(1/3)
'One third is: 0.333'
>>> # string alignment
>>> "|{:<10}|{:^10}|{:>10}|".format('butter','bread','ham')
'|butter    |  bread   |       ham|'
```

Old style formatting

We even can code strings such as the old sprint() style in the programming language used in C. To accomplish this; we use the '%' operator.

```
>>> x = 12.3456789

>>>print('The value of x is %3.2f' %x)

The value of x is 12.35

>>>print('The value of x is %3.4f' %x)

The value of x is 12.3457
```

String common Methods for Python

The string object comes with various methods. One of them is the format() method we described above. A few other frequently used technique include lower(), upper(), join(), split(), find(), substitute() etc. Here is a wide-range list of several of the built-in methodologies in Python for working with strings.

```
>>> "PrOgRaMiZ".lower()

'programiz'

>>> "PrOgRaMiZ".upper()

'PROGRAMIZ'

>>> "This will split all words into a list".split()

['This', 'will', 'split', 'all', 'words', 'into', 'a', 'list']

>>> ' '.join(['This', 'will', 'join', 'all', 'words', 'into', 'a', 'string'])

'This will join all words into a string'

>>> 'Happy New Year'.find('ew')

7

>>> 'Happy New Year'.replace('Happy','Brilliant')

'Brilliant New Year'
```

Inserting values into strings

Method 1 - the string format method

The string method format method can be used to create new strings with the values inserted. That method works for all of Python's recent releases. That is where we put a string in another string:

```
>>>shepherd = "Mary"

>>>string_in_string = "Shepherd {} is on duty.".format(shepherd)

>>>print(string_in_string)
```

Shepherd Mary is on duty.

The curved braces indicate where the inserted value will be going.

You can insert a value greater than one. The values should not have to be strings; numbers and other Python entities may be strings.

```
>>>shepherd = "Mary"
>>>age = 32
>>>stuff_in_string = "Shepherd {} is {} years old.".format(shepherd, age)
>>>print(stuff_in_string)
Shepherd Mary is 32 years old.
>>> 'Here is a {} floating point number'.format(3.33333)
'Here is a 3.33333 floating point number'
```

Using the formatting options within curly brackets, you can do more complex formatting of numbers and strings — see the information on curly brace string layout.

This process allows us to give instructions for formatting things such as numbers, using either: inside the curly braces, led by guidance for formatting. Here we request you to print in integer (d) in which the number is 0 to cover the field size of 3:

```
>>>print("Number {:03d} is here.".format(11))

Number 011 is here.

This prints a floating point value (f) with exactly 4 digits after the decimal point

>>> 'A formatted number - {:.4f}'.format(.2)

'A formatted number - 0.2000'
```

Method 2 - f-strings in Python >= 3.6

When you can rely on having Python > = version 3.6, you will have another appealing place to use the new literal (f-string) formatted string to input variable values. Just at the start of the string, an f informs Python to permit any presently valid variable names inside the string as column names. So here's an example such as the one above, for instance using the f-string syntax:

```
>>>shepherd = "Martha"

>>>age = 34

>>> # Note f before first quote of string

>>>stuff_in_string = f"Shepherd {shepherd} is {age} years old."

>>>print(stuff_in_string)
```

Shepherd Martha is 34 years old.

Method 3 - old school % formatting

There seems to be an older string formatting tool, which uses the percent operator. It is a touch less versatile than the other two choices, but you can still see it in use in older coding, where it is more straightforward to use '%' formatting. For formatting the '%' operator, you demonstrate where the encoded values should go using a '%' character preceded by a format identifier to tell how to add the value.

So here's the example earlier in this thread, using formatting by '%.' Note that '%s' marker for a string to be inserted, and the '%d' marker for an integer.

```
>>>stuff_in_string = "Shepherd %s is %d years old." % (shepherd, age)
>>>print(stuff_in_string)
```
Shepherd Martha is 34 years old.

MODULE DATA

―――――――○―――――――

What are the modules in Python?

Whenever you leave and re-enter the Python interpreter, the definitions you have created (functions and variables) will get lost. Consequently, if you'd like to develop a code a little longer, it's better to use a text editor to plan the input for the interpreter and execute it with that file as input conversely. This is defined as script formation. As the software gets bigger, you may want to break it into different files to make maintenance simpler. You might also like to use a handy function that you wrote in many other programs without having to replicate its definition inside each program. To assist this, Python has the option of putting definitions into a file and using them in the interpreter's code or interactive instances. This very file is considered a module; module descriptions can be loaded into certain modules or into the main module (the list of variables you have exposure to in a high-level script and in converter mode).

A module is a file that contains definitions and statements from Python. The name of the file is the name of the module with the .py suffix attached. The name of the module (only as string) inside a module is available as the value, including its global variable __name__. For example, use your preferred text editor to build a file named fibo.py with the following contents in the current working directory:

```
# Python Module example

def add(a, b):

    """This program adds two

numbers and return the result"""

result = a + b

return result
```

In this, we defined an add() function within an example titled " module." The function requires two numbers and returns a total of them.

How to import modules in Python?

Within a module, we can import the definitions to some other module or even to the interactive Python interpreter. To do something like this, we use the keyword import. To load our recently specified example module, please enter in the Python prompt.

>>> import example

This should not import the identities of the functions directly in the existing symbol table, as defined in the example. It just imports an example of the module name there.

Using the name of the module, we can use the dot(.) operator to access the function. For instance:

>>>example.add(4,5.5)

9.5

Python comes with lots of regular modules. Check out the complete list of regular Python modules and their usage scenarios. These directories are within the destination where you've installed Python in the Lib directory. Normal modules could be imported just the same as our user-defined modules are imported.

There are different ways of importing the modules. You'll find them below:

Python import statement

Using the import statement, we can extract a module by using the dot operator, as explained in the previous section and access the definitions within it. Here is another example.

```
# import statement example

# to import standard module math

import math

print("The value of pi is", math.pi)
```

Once we execute the code above, we have the following results:

The value of pi is 3.141592653589793

Import with renaming

We can load a module in the following way by changing the name of it:

```
# import module by renaming it

import math as m

print("The value of pi is", m.pi)
```

We called the module Math as m. In certain instances, this will save us time to type. Remember that in our scope, the name math is not identified. Therefore math.pi is incorrect, and m.pi is correctly implemented.

Python from...import statement

We can import individual names from such a module without having to import the entire module. Here is another example.

```
# import only pi from math module

from math import pi

print("The value of pi is", pi)
```

In this, only the pi parameter was imported from the math module. We don't utilize the dot operator in certain cases. We can likewise import different modules:

>>>from math import pi, e

>>>pi

3.141592653589793

>>>e

2.718281828459045

Import all names

With the following form, we can import all terms (definitions) from a module:

import all names from standard module math

from math import *

print("The value of pi is," pi)

Above, we have added all of the math module descriptions. This covers all names that are available in our scope except those that start with an underscore. It is not a good programming technique to import something with the asterisk (*) key. This will lead to a replication of an attribute's meaning. This also restricts our code's readability.

Python Module Search Path

Python looks at many locations when importing a module. Interpreter searches for a built-in module instead. So if not included in the built-in module, Python searches at a collection of directories specified in sys.path. The exploration is in this sequence:

PYTHONPATH (list of directories environment variable)

The installation-dependent default directory

```
>>> import sys

>>>sys.path

['',

'C:\\Python33\\Lib\\idlelib',

'C:\\Windows\\system32\\python33.zip',

'C:\\Python33\\DLLs',

'C:\\Python33\\lib',

'C:\\Python33',

'C:\\Python33\\lib\\site-packages']
```

We can insert that list and customize it to insert our own location.

Reloading a module

During a session, the Python interpreter needs to import one module only once. This makes matters more productive. Here is an example showing how that operates.

Assume we get the code below in a module called my_module:

```
# This module shows the effect of

#  multiple imports and reload

print("This code got executed")
```

Now we suspect that multiple imports have an impact.

```
>>> import my_module
```

This code was executed:

>>> import my_module

>>> import my_module

We have seen our code was only executed once. This means that our module has only been imported once.

Also, if during the process of the test our module modified, we will have to restart it. The way to do so is to reload the interpreter. But that doesn't massively help. Python offers an effective way to do so. Within the imp module, we may use the reload() function to restart a module. Here are some ways to do it:

>>> import imp

>>> import my_module

This code executes

>>> import my_module

>>>imp.reload(my_module)

This code executes

<module 'my_module' from '.\\my_module.py'>

The dir() built-in function

We may use the dir() function to locate names specified within a module. For such cases, in the example of the module that we had in the early part, we described a function add().

In example module, we can use dir in the following scenario:

```
>>>dir(example)
['__builtins__',
'__cached__',
'__doc__',
'__file__',
'__initializing__',
'__loader__',
'__name__',
'__package__',
'add']
```

Now we'll see a list of the names sorted (alongside add). Many other names that start with an underscore are module-associated (not user-defined) default Python attributes. For instance, the attribute name contains module __name__.

```
>>> import example
>>>example.__name__
'example'
```

You can find out all names identified in our existing namespace by using dir() function with no arguments.

```
>>> a = 1
>>> b = "hello"
>>> import math
>>>dir()
['__name__', '__doc__','__builtins__ ', 'a', 'b', 'math', 'pyscripter']
```

Executing modules as scripts

Python module running with python fibo.py <arguments>the program will be running in such a way, just like it was being imported, but including the __name__ set to "__main__." That implies this program is inserted at the end of the module:

If __name__ == "__main__": import sys fib(int(sys.argv[1]))

You could even create the file usable both as a script and as an importable module since this code parsing the command - line interface runs only when the module is performed as the "main" file:

$ python fibo.py 50

0 1 1 2 3 5 8 13

When the module is imported, the code will not be executed:

>>>

>>> import fibo

>>>

It is most often used whether to get an efficient user interface to a module or for test purposes (the module runs a test suite as a script).

"Compiled" Python files

To speed up loading modules, Python caches the compiled version of each module in the __pycache__ directory with the name module.version.pyc, in which the version encapsulates the assembled file format; it normally includes the firmware version of Python. For instance, the compiled edition of spam.py in CPython launch 3.3 will be cached as __pycache__/spam.cpython-33.pyc. This naming convention enables the coexistence of compiled modules from various updates and separate versions of Python.

Python tests the source change schedule against the compiled edition to see if it is out-of-date and needs recompilation. That's a fully automated system. Even the assembled modules become platform-independent, so different algorithms will use the same library between systems. In two situations Pythoniswill not check the cache:

➤ First, it often recompiles the output for the module, which is loaded explicitly from the command line but does not store it.
➤ Second, when there is no root module, it will not search the cache. The compiled module must be in the source directory to facilitate a non-source (compiled only) release, and a source module should not be installed.

Some tips for users:

• To minimize the size of a compiled file, you can use the -O or -OO switches in the Python order. The -O switch erases statements of assert, the -OO switch removes statements of assert as well as strings of doc. Although some codes may support getting these options available, this method should only be used if you are aware of what you are doing. "Optimized" modules usually have such an opt-tag and are tinier. Future releases may modify the optimal control implications.

- A project run no faster once it is read from a.pyc file than how it was read from a.py file; just one thing about.pyc files that are faster in the speed with which they will be loaded.
- A compile all modules can generate .pyc files in a directory for all of the other modules.
- More details on this process are given in PEP 3147, along with a flow chart of the decision making.

Standard Modules

Python has a standard modules library, mentioned in a separate section, the Python Library allusion (hereafter "Library Reference"). A few modules are incorporated into the interpreter; that provide direct exposure to processes that are not component of the language's base but are nonetheless built-in, whether for effectiveness or to supply access to primitive operating systems such as source code calls. The collection of these modules is an alternative to customize and also relies on the framework underlying it. The winreg module, for instance, is only available on Microsoft windows. One particular module is worthy of certain interest: sys, which is integrated into every Python interpreter. The sys.ps1 and sys.ps2 variables classify strings which are used as primary and secondary instructions:

```
>>>

>>> import sys

>>> sys.ps1

'>>> '

>>> sys.ps2

'... '
```

```
>>> sys.ps1 = 'C> '
```

```
C>print('Yuck!')
```

Yuck!

```
C>
```

Only when the interpreter is in interactive mode are those two variables defined. The sys.path variable is a collection of strings that defines the search path for modules used by the interpreter. When PYTHONPATH is not a part of the set, then it will be defined to a predefined path taken from either the PYTHONPATH environment variable or through a built-in default. You can change it with regular list procedures:

```
>>>
```

```
>>> import sys
```

```
>>>sys.path.append('/python/ufs/guido/lib/')
```

Packages

Packages are indeed a way to construct the namespace of the Python module by using "pointed names of the module." For instance, in a package called A., the module title A.B specifies a submodule named B. Even as the use of modules prevents the writers of various modules from stopping to know about the global variable names of one another, any use of dotted module names prevents the developers of multi-module bundles like NumPy or Pillow from needing to worry more about module names of one another. Consider making a series of lists of modules (a "package") to handle sound files and sound data in an even manner.

There are several various programs of sound files usually familiar with their extension, for example: 'wav,.aiff,.au,' though you'll need to build and maintain a massive collection of modules to convert between some of the multiple formats of files. There are several other different operations that you may like to run on sound data (such as blending, adding echo, implementing an equalizer function, producing an optical stereo effect), and you'll just be writing an infinite series of modules to execute those interventions. Here is another feasible package layout (described in terms of a hierarchical file system):

```
sound/                          Top level package
        __init__.py                 sound package initialization
formats/                        Subpackage for conversions of file format
                __init__.py
                wavread.py
                wavwrite.py
                aiffread.py
                aiffwrite.py
                auread.py
                auwrite.py
                ...
effects/                        Sound effectssubpackage
                __init__.py
                echo.py
                surround.py
                reverse.py
                ...
filters/                        Filterssubpackage
                __init__.py
                equalizer.py
                vocoder.py
                karaoke.py
                ...
```

While loading the bundle, Python checks for the packet subdirectory via the folders on sys.path. To allow Python view directories that hold the file as packages, the __init__.py files are needed. This protects directories with a common name, including string, from accidentally hiding valid modules, which later appear mostly on the search path of the module. In the correct order; __init__.py can only be a blank file, but it could also implement the package preprocessing code or establish the variable __all__ described below

o Package users could even upload individual modules from the package, such as: 'import sound.effects.echo'
o This loads the 'sound.effects.echo' sub-module. Its full name must be mentioned: 'sound.effects.echo.echofilter(input, output, atten=4, delay=0.7)'
o Another way to import the submodule is: 'fromsound.effects import echo'
o It, therefore, launches the sub-module echo and provides access but without package prefix: 'echo.echofilter(input, output, atten=4, delay=0.7)'
o And just another option is to explicitly import the desired function or attribute: 'fromsound.effects.echo import echofilter'
o This again activates the echo sub-module however this enables its echofilter() feature explicitly accessible: 'echofilter(input, output, delay=0.7, atten=4)'

So it heaps the sub-module echo; however this tends to make its function; remember that the object will either be a sub-module (or sub-package)of the package or any other name described in the package, such as a function, class or variable while using from package import object. Initially, the import statement analyses if the object is characterized in the package; otherwise, it supposes that it is a module and makes an attempt to load it. Once it fails to reach it, an exception to 'ImportError' will be promoted.

Referring to this, while using syntax such as import 'item.subitem.subsubitem', each item has to be a package, but the last one; the last item could be a module or package, but this cannot be a class or function or variable identified in the previous item.

CONCLUSION

Research across almost all fields has become more data-oriented, impacting both the job opportunities and the required skills. While more data and methods of evaluating them are becoming obtainable, more data-dependent aspects of the economy, society, and daily life are becoming. Whenever it comes to data science, Python is a tool necessary with all sorts of advantages. It is flexible and continually improving because it is open-source. Python already has a number of valuable libraries, and it cannot be ignored that it can be combined with other languages (like Java) and current frameworks. Long story short -Python is an amazing method for data science.

www.ingramcontent.com/pod-product-compliance
Lightning Source LLC
LaVergne TN
LVHW051742050326
832903LV00029B/2663